the flap pamphlet series

Portrait of Colossus

open, read, turn

Portrait of Colossus

the flap pamphlet series (No. 22)
Printed and Bound in the United Kingdom

Published by the flap series, 2021
the pamphlet series of flipped eye publishing
All Rights Reserved

Cover Design by Petraski
Series Design © flipped eye publishing, 2010

Author Photo © Samatar Elmi/Stewart Baxter
First Edition
Copyright © Samatar Elmi 2021
#JusticeForShurkriAbdi

ISBN: 978-1-905233-61-8

Supported using public funding by
**ARTS COUNCIL
ENGLAND**
LOTTERY FUNDED

Portrait of Colossus

Samatar Elmi

Contents | *Portrait of Colossus*

Portrait of Colossus as an Immigrant.............................7
Diaspora 8
The Invaders 9
England..10
Manuel Cortes and the Immortal Tree...............................11
Step This Way 13
NIGGER..14
The End of History..15
Cassandra's Dream 16
Etudes 17
From a Father to a Daughter 20
Burqa...22
The Hope and Anchor...23
Drunk on Rūm..24
Marbles 25
Manhood 26
When I Think of Nostalgia I Think of Bramble Picking 27
Orpheus as a Busker...28
Cain and Abel 29
Mirrors...30
Paradise 31
On Cash Machines and Supermarkets.................................32
Khat House 33
Your Mother is in a Different Language 34

Portrait of Colossus as an Immigrant
after Plath

I picture him fixed in stride across wandering oceans;
a bridge, reluctant between immovable banks,

wedged like a fallen tree, an angel.

It's a footing that keeps him sentinel and sleepless,
knowing a slip in the east is all it takes

to bring him to his knees, then face-down into Rome.

I want to scale his limbs;
sit in the brass of his ear,

whisper on the similitudes of the world. How
at such great heights all language is a blur,
people indistinguishable as fields of corn, sand...

But he's all eyes on the water,

its movement and liberty;

the trick of being everywhere at once.

Diaspora

For Hadraawi

If poetry should remain our propagule,
what is the language of Diaspora?
Teach us a poem of infinite translation:

help us reach beyond our confines
like the wind that ripped us from the maple

and scattered us on winged samara
from Amsterdam to Oklahoma,
in the ever-spreading shadows of our Babel.

The Invaders

"England must be reconquered for the English.
They should go back from whence they came."
— John Townend (Former Conservative MP)

I am parrot's feather, pennywort
water fern and primrose.
I am the susurrus of grey squirrels

in the branches by your windows.

I carry crayfish plague through fenland
wash and highland stream.

My thick roots tear at the bedrock
under country lane and tower block.

I am a London gang of parakeet;

the coypus close to you as skin.
The sand that beds your cobbled streets,
things will never be the same again.

England

In lieu of a detailed taxonomy,
the names of trees I camped beside;
in lieu of a firm footing
is the solemn recognition

that I know you
more than everywhere else
put together.

Not quite belonging, but
the closest I will come
to finding my home
is walking alone at end of the night

over Parliament bridge
past Nelson's column
up to Camden,

up and up,
until at Hampstead
where the first impressions of dawn
are the songs of birds

whose names
I never had to learn
for them to sing for me.

Manuel Cortes and the Immortal Tree

At first I was amused
by these little trees
kept by little people.

I followed the ghosts of Cabral,
Columbus and de Gama
for the promise of immortality.

I found a tree as old as Rome
and a master with a taste for deadwood,
a passion for grey ropes coiling and matting
the trunk, wide brooms and ball crowns;
an eye for grafting fragile species onto firmer roots.
I preferred the chokkan bonsai, the formal upright style.

It reminded me of Lisbon,
before the earthquake,
the horrors of the untamed.

No storm has ever harmed the masters
training their bonsai into form;
a forest of akadama bowls.

I came to admire the bonsai's talent
for twisting around guide wires
into something foreseeable.
And how a master exploits
the bonsai's daily thirst for light,
each lean preceded by a desire to lean,

the bonsai learning through careful pruning
the master's art, his quest to live
vicariously through undying wood

The secret is letting the trees believe
they're not dwarfs, rather
we are giants.

Step This Way

When asked to step this way
you'll fear that the look of *not again*
will scream guilty, bring out the mugshot
in your babyface; those distant dilated eyes
hauling their weight like a porter:
false testimonies, the betrayal of friends.

Don't resist. Just step their way
into a world of hidden accusations. Engage,
however painful, in their polite interrogations
dressed as the small talk of *why this flight,
this destination*. Ignore the unease of fellow
passengers; the empty seats beside us.

Whatever you do, don't bark
I've stepped your way my whole life;
let's face it, you look the part
black/brown, 5'4" to 6'6", dreadlocks
to balding to bearded to bomb. *Please*.
Don't be quick with *I'm an Englishman*.

Why should they believe you?
You scarcely believe it yourself.

NIGGER

"Rappers when you use the word "nigger"
remember that's one of the last words Stephen Lawrence heard,
so don't tell me it's a reclaimed word."
— Dean Atta

Taken out of context, six black letters
on a white page, a word with Latin
                    not African roots.

The many Roman synonyms;
taeter, malificus, piceus.

Morum: the black mulberry fruit.
Atratus: clothed in black.

But *nigrum* made its way to us.
Its two syllables a kick and snare.

The front stress a gut punch, low
blow knocking the wind out of you.

A schwa hangs limp behind,
like still fruit from the branch

and in that violence
in the midst of all the violence

vowels are choked
the 'I' suffocated

even when taken out of context. .

The End of History

I had for many years forgotten the night
the Greatest Circus in the World
performed its greatest trick,
packing itself away into mucky crates
and disappearing before dawn.

Tonight, all I can remember is that circus
as I watch our country fold into folds
like a scrunched-up map
and wonder about that old trick
the sleight of hand, the puff of smoke.

Cassandra's Dream

There was always that dream of running
to shop for mum; the uneventfulness,
the illusion of being awake with every step

– like the weight of my rucksack,
a gluey heat building in my cap,
the slip of shit beneath the shoe –

only to return to a home
no longer ours, a stranger
standing in the kitchen
teeth grinding in the lock.

Except I always wake up
before the neighbours speak
a silence that splits the ground

and gobbles up the Earth.

Etudes

i.
You will never know the measure of things
until you let go of the strings that strap you in
like once in the life of an acorn
to nosedive, blindly through the air.
And just like the acorn you'll never
know your place until you land.

ii.
To see you all bleeps, tubes and catheters,
kept alive where the slightest cough could
tip the balance, was harder than whispering
what I knew and didn't know you could hear.

iii.
Every poem should start with soon, my love.
Soon kept us going in winter.
Soon is the prayer of the broken.
Soon is a father's favourite word.
And soon, my love, you might realise
that I never started this poem with soon;
what does that say, now my love?

iv.
The last man to pray
will not ask for guidance
for signs or forgiveness
not even wealth and glory.
The last man to pray will ask
how can I tell if I'm alive?

v.
After seven years, I placed it filter-end,
                    between my lips and it felt
like the first sip of water in the morning,
                    like rain on a glacier.

vi.
and so I set myself upon this path
that leads to Saigon, to the burning monk,
to ask him how it was to feel nothing
and everything at once?

vii.
There are sketches we find in notepads
years old and out of body
half-poems abandoned in boxes and drawers,
that remind us that even unrequited love
is generous with its gifts.

viii.
Once, I set out to stop the shaman.
His burning tower. His evil eye.
I didn't know which loss was worse
my limbs or injuries, only
that I was losing, and losing
the will to keep losing.

And the Lord said
you are either tested or blessed;
blessed when your tested
tested when your blessed
and a curse is what you make
between yourselves.
The will to keep losing

that I had lost, when I lost
my limbs and injuries, only
I didn't know which loss was worse.
My burning tower. My evil eye.
Once I set out to stop the shaman.

ix.
Can I still remember what it felt like
my heart of Alpine water?

Forgive us our trespasses
and deliver us from evil

Ameen.

From a Father to a Daughter

( )

Your mother wants poems about you;
fatherhood-bildungsroman-eulogies,
cleaver villanelles, where like you, the refrain
reinvents the stanzas of our narrative,
a reassuring haven for us to return to.
She wants sonnets that mirror the paradox
between finite space and infinite odds,
fit for you, our living breathing dialectic.
But I haven't any poems, save fragments
that can't hold a candle to the lyric
of your light and yet I try and try
to find a box that can hold the Sun.

♬

Once, I lived in semi-quavers, alternating
rhythm – spiral waltzes and dizzy 5/4,
a mid-eight that passed like an absence seizure,
the fruits of a cherry glowing in an overgrown
ashtray, self-flagellation by eight-track mixers
and shit EQs, the torture of striking a balance
with little more than an out of tune piano.
Miriam, you're too young to understand now,
but you're the breve in every bar, pianississimo,
the gift of common time for a mind in syncopation.
You are chronograph, sundial, my crutch -
your voice carries the libretto to our opera.
I swear to God you're too young to understand,
mother of my harmony, my anno domini.

π.

I am your father but you made me a son.
I held your hands as we learned to walk.
Your first parroted words reimagined
my lexicon, the imbued semiotics
of *dada, mama, Mimi* – no longer a string
of morphemes but the first bricks of Babel
where we built our modest temple.

Your gargled gagaga, which we learned
was the purest expression of love -
became our prayer at the altar.

Now you decorate the walls of our temple
with icons, scribbles, our family in sticks
as if to hold our hands through the growing

and teach us both how to write a poem.

Burqa

The ink has rubbed from her copies
of *Canopus in Argos, Gravity and Grace*.
She reads verses from *The Second Sex*,
ad libs rhythm, pitch and tone
until this quaint and very English imam
crescendos with the cadences
of *Iqra Bismi Rabbika*:

> One is not born, but rather
> becomes, a woman.

She scolds her brothers for their sins:
as bachelors; their western laissez-faire,
hides their razors in the morning
in case they forget the beard is *fard*,
along with the *thobe* to guard
their nakedness. They nod,
knowing she will tell them:

> To lose confidence in one's body
> is to lose confidence in oneself.

Then there's the daily invite to amble
publicly where the broad daylight smacks
against the jet black burqa:
and oh how the boys fear
that people will think they forced her.
And now to their unspoken mantra;
if only they knew her.

The Hope and Anchor

An imam stands where the last barmaid called last orders,
his jukebox of aythaan and ayaat, his little number.
Worshippers squeeze into rank and row - face Mecca -
as once punters, rasping for that one-for-the-road,
made a beeline for the last pitcher. Now empty beerlines,
still clipped to walls, snake to a cellar parched with prohibition.
Where once the fount was stocked with cask and cork –
now a beer garden bench for alif, baa, taa...

Stalagmites reach for the ghost of a liquor bottle rack;
you can hear the ghost of Jim Beam through the palimpsest.
And a wooden sign above the door: *The Hope and Anchor*,
which the imam kept - a portly reminder that God's house
is *al-amal wa marsa*, that others have gathered here to escape
until last orders.

ayaat – verse in the Quran
aythaan – call to prayer
alif, baa, taa – first three letters of the Arabic alphabet
al-amal wa marsa – the hope and anchor.

Drunk on Rūm

Our parents are disappointed.
They raised us right. Right,
I remind them, in the shadow
of the Colosseum.

I hate that I was looking up.
But, father, how can one be sober
gazing at the Eiffel Tower, pissed
as a fart in the British Museum?

Rūm – Romans in Arabic

Marbles

What they don't tell you about the kids on the estate,
are the marble collections, all the invention
of kids who make a hundred games out of nothing.

Except they're not nothing, are they, these marbles?
In the right hands they can be anything
- ancient relics, priceless jewels.

Planets in the tiny hands of titans.

And one by one we have them taken from us.
Confiscated in schools,
a safety hazard

- some of us learn to hide them,

or think we've hidden them,
not daring to look inside purses
that haven't been opened in years;

just giving the bag a shake from time to time,
only to find ourselves doubting again
whether the clack clack was ever really there at all.

Manhood

He never gave much away
but I always knew he was under it

when a cigarette filled the silence.
The entire stick pulled in a couple of draws.

Two inches of flaming coal tip-to-filter
and not a speck of ash

- a sort of controlled demolition:

the paper squeezing like a diaphragm,
his eyes flat out on the pavement.

When I Think of Nostalgia I Think of Bramble Picking

It will always be autumn
when clocks go back an hour
and conkers stew into molasses -
rain-swelled in spoiling leaves
along miles of coppered railings.
The sky doubled-over, full-term,
sprays an imperceptible mist
that plumps the blackberries
and holds a thousand refractions
to catch our eye - autumn,
always less about the harvest
than the ritual – its pudding
of reminiscence – the never-fading
bitter-sweet, the empty baking tray.

Orpheus as a Busker

"Belief in God is no longer axiomatic. There are alternatives.
And this will also likely mean that at least in certain milieux,
it may be hard to sustain one's faith."
        – Charles Taylor

He doesn't do it for spare change lobbed into his lap;
he plays to regain the power to halt coins in mid-air
like back in the day when his lyre could out-do Sirens.
He doesn't do it for small talk or drunken sing-alongs;

he strums away assured of his comeback; certain
that he'll be found in a mixolydian mix of notes,
his food for Muses. He plays on a prayer that Zeus
will reappear and end the moratorium on magic,

that one day this marginal busker, armed with his music
will repair the disenchantment, make us all believe again.

Cain and Abel

The first time I met my country of origin
I fell flat on my face and kissed the ground so hard
the sand bit my lips. This is how my country returns affection.

A love that is proved in the mixture
of blood, sand and saliva.
Where ventriloquism is practised
not as art but artifice.
It would be years before I would also learn
the semantics of glares and glances.

> Family, they say, is fixed by unseen ribbons
> blood, blood money and gravity.
> But what about the lies
> that drained rivers, mixed salt into seas,
> stripped the flora down to this barren, burning allegory?

For years I would prove my commitment
in this trial of endurance – never daring to ask
how much longer can I grit my teeth?
The gravel of enamel, bits of gum and cheek,
like Cain's unworthy sacrifice.
I never asked myself
have I reached their measure?

> Except that more is the only measure.
> And when at last you open wide
> who will look beyond the charred stubs of teeth
> to see into the night they fashioned
> the faint *hilal* barely registering
> beneath the North star that has always dragged you back.

Hilal – crescent moon

29

Mirrors

This poem is a mirror
I've made for us, Hadraawi,
A mirror we can hold up
To show the fool
The depth of self-deception
That lies in his reflection.
                    Gaariye

In this wilderness of mirrors /
we become an image refracted in a stagnant pool / a Penderecki master-
piece of madness / crescendos of echoes made all the more familiar
by talk of the good old days // Can't you see that we are trapped (trapped
are we that see, you can't?) / in a perfect feedback loop / in an Escher
diagram / that we walk
up and down the stairs to nowhere /
in this wilderness of mirrors?

Paradise

On nights we need reminding of our luck,
let's follow in the spirit of the Abyssinian bloke
who lived in our much-maligned tower block,
walked through corridors wound like a souk,
past hutches, hot boxes, through smoke and mist,
the felt-tip tags and murals, the pissed-
up in stairwells, the piss stench of steps,
the wrinkled johnnies, abandoned creps.

Recall how he tapped you on the shoulder
pointing to the lights beyond the balcony,
convinced that the city was in the eye of the beholder.
Recall his description of the Great Rift Valley,
how the infinite horizon is an incarceration,
how one man's paradise is another's prison.

On Cash Machines and Supermarkets

"No one leaves home unless home is the mouth of a shark"
– Warsan Shire

i.
I asked the seabed about my cousin who died
learning how to swim, and would the ocean
be so kind as to bury him, and would a marlin
lead the prayer as they placed him in his kaffan

I weighted down a muslin sheet with rocks
and threw it off Berbera pier, and wondered
what it was that brought me here: survivor's guilt,
Stockholm syndrome, or simply the fear of water?

ii.
I happened to be born in a wonderland
green with rain, where even the walls
are charitable. A land of banquet halls and feasting,
and rows and rows of onions, manna and quails,
where if all else fails there is the freedom
from the fear of fear itself.

iii.
But another child threatens to walk to heaven,
and I don't know how to play it down -
that even if you could swim, the seabed
might be an afterlife, but it ain't a paradise.

So I start with the old Faustian trade
about a bargain that never ends well.
But who cares about the flaws of paradise,
that ATMs and supermarkets come at a price?

Khat House

The elders hold counsel, every night, in a burning house.
We are numb to the flames, so we talk.
Over time, fire has become our favourite metaphor.

We all agree that the West is a fire; warm, vital, fatal –
so we ponder *an-naar*: how forest fires, solar flares,
candle light and Mogadishu are notes of a mode.

One elder speaks of the women who birth snakes
that prophesy fire for forty years, or ten generations,
(depending on the version). Still, the promise of fire

tricks the mind into believing that the flames purify,
that we are somehow, through all this talk, still Abrahamic.
That somehow, through all this talk, we are good.

And that's all it takes to ignore
the quiet glow of khat leaves, its soft crepitation,
the smoke slowly rising in the room.

Your Mother is in a Different Language

*"The words of this language are to refer to what can be known only to
the speaker; to his immediate, private, sensations. So another cannot
understand the language."*
— Ludwig Wittgenstein

Your mother is in a different language.
It didn't matter when she took her oath
of burden, placenta and breast milk,

her promise of patience and insomnia
that she clung to for seven thousand nights
of drifting in and out of speechlessness.
No one saw the nurse sever the umbilical cord,
your first and last line of unbroken communication
tossed into a medical waste bin;
the doctor muttering faint instructions in English
for the nurse to rock you asleep with lullabies
your mother couldn't understand.

No one thought it odd that mother and son
should bring a translator to parents' evening
to bridge between their broken tongues.
The swirling cacophony of waar muxuu leeyahay
and what's she on about making it easier
to just kiss her forehead in silence.
How did you get here, fifteen years of false starts,
sat together in a courtroom, an unbridgeable gulf,
your mother shaking, shaping words like a prayer?
Except that hooyo, hooyo, maxaad samaysay?
isn't a prayer – it's a question you can't answer
in a language she understands.

*Hooyo, hooyo, maxaad samaysay – roughly equivalent to 'my son, my son, what
have you done'.*
waar muxuu leeyahay - roughly equivalent to 'what is he saying'